Oxford University Press, Walton Street, Oxford OX2 6DP

Oxford   New York   Toronto
Delhi   Bombay   Calcutta   Madras   Karachi
Petaling Jaya   Singapore   Hong Kong   Tokyo
Nairobi   Dar es Salaam   Cape Town
Melbourne   Auckland

and associated companies in
Berlin   Ibadan

Oxford is a trade mark of Oxford University Press

© Word Rhymes: Roger McGough 1990
© Text: Dee Reid 1990
First edition 1990
Reprinted 1990 ,1991,1992
First published in paperback 1991
Reprinted 1992

ISBN 0 19 910247 3 (Hardback)
ISBN 0 19 910260 0 (Paperback)

Typeset by Tradespools Limited, Frome, Somerset
Printed in Belgium

Parents' notes

This fun-filled activity dictionary has so much to keep children amused while they are learning.

Each double page has a beautifully illustrated picture packed full of items beginning with a letter of the alphabet. There is a wealth of detail for readers of all ages to pore over.

Each page also has a puzzle activity, a joke and some silhouettes to identify.

The dictionary entries each have their own little picture and an accompanying phrase or rhyme. These have been devised to cater for children's fascination with the sound that words make.

Children will enjoy getting their tongues round the humorous verses and this playing with rhyme is the perfect preparation for becoming a reader.

Younger children will enjoy finding the ten listed items in amongst the busy large picture.

Older children (and adults!) might like to search to find the many extra items that begin with each particular letter. You will find a checklist of the illustrated items at the back of the book.

This book can be dipped into and enjoyed on many occasions and in many ways. It offers an early introduction to alphabet order and a delightful means of expanding a child's vocabulary.

a b c d e f g h i j k l m n o p q r s t u v w x y z

Angry ants, adorable aunts
Angular anchors aweigh
Active acrobats, acorns and apples
Alligators (all A).

acorn
An acre of acorns

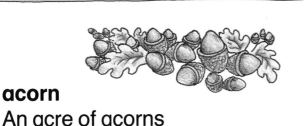

ant
A line of angry ants

acrobat
An active acrobat

antelope
The antelope ran up the slope.

alligator
An agitated alligator

apple
A juicy apple

alphabet
I bet you know your alphabet.

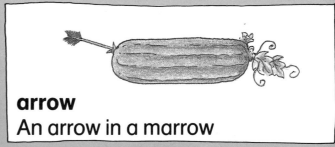

arrow
An arrow in a marrow

anchor
The heavy anchor sank her.

astronaut
An astronaut out for a walk.

Aa

See you later alligator.

In a while crocodile.

Use the stepping stones to hop along the alphabet path.

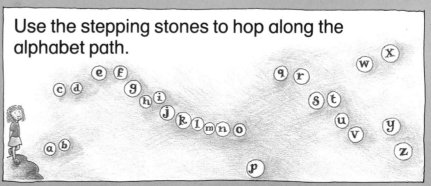

a b c d e f g h i j k l m n o p q r s t u v w x y z

Say 'Hello' to Bill Buffalo
On his bicycle there.
Best balancer in the business
Better than any bear.

baby
A bouncing baby

bicycle
Can you ride a bicycle?

badger
Don't badger a badger.

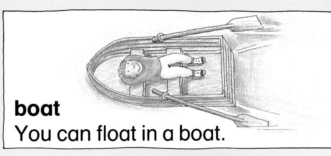

boat
You can float in a boat.

balloon
The balloon popped.

bulldozer
A bulldog in a bulldozer

bear
A hairy bear

bus
A double-decker bus

bee
Buzzing bees

butterfly
A butterfly fluttered by.

Bb

What do you call a sleeping bull?

A bulldozer.

Use the **b** in the balloon to make some words.

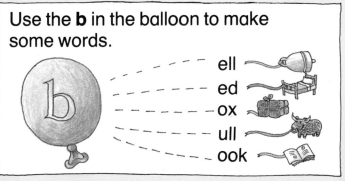

ell
ed
ox
ull
ook

a b c d e f g h i j k l m n o p q r s t u v w x y z

They are building an escalator
Up Mount Everest they say
So that mountaineers like us
Can conquer it each day.

eagle
An eagle in its eyrie

engine
A car engine

ear
You hear with your ears.

envelope
A letter in an envelope

eel
As slippery as an eel

escalator
An alligator on an escalator

egg
Would you expect
an egg to explode?

exit
An extra exit

elephant
Eleven elephants

eye
I saw his eye was sore.

Ee 11

Why do elephants have trunks?

They'd look funny with suitcases, wouldn't they?

A ewe is a mother sheep. Find babies for each of these mothers:

cow   duck   cat   frog

a b c d e f g h i j k l m n o p q r s t u v w x y z

Here comes a hamster with a hammer
Hide the nail
The last time he played handyman
He hurt his tail.

hammer
A hammer and nails

helmet
A fireman's helmet

hamster
A hamster in a cage

hippopotamus
A happy hippo

harp
A carp playing the harp

house
A house for a mouse

hedgehog
A tickly, prickly hedgehog

hovercraft
The hovercraft
laughed at the raft.

helicopter
A rescue helicopter

hutch
Who lives in a hutch?

Hh

What do you get when you cross a giraffe with a hedgehog?

An 11 metre hairbrush.

Humpty Dumpty sat on a ▨▨▨ had a great fall.
All the King's 🐎🐎🐎
and all the King's 💂💂💂
Couldn't put 🥚 together again.

a b c d e f g h i j k l m n o p q r s t u v w x y z

The kangaroo is the king of karate
(His belt is black)
Kicking quarrelsome kids at a party
(They'll not come back.)

kangaroo
The kangaroo has lost his shoe.

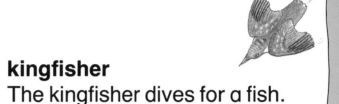

kingfisher
The kingfisher dives for a fish.

kennel
Who sleeps in this kennel?

kitten
Can you count the kittens?

key
He kept the key in the ketchup.

knife
Who knows where a knight
keeps his knife?

kilt
He spilt his milk on his kilt.

knitting
The kitten was sitting
on the knitting.

king
The king wore a ring.

koala
Carla kept a koala in the parlour.

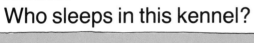

Kk

What's this?

A koala climbing up a tree.

Help the kangaroo to jump along the number path.

 ② ④ ⑥ ⑨
① ③ ⑤ ⑦ ⑧ ⑩

Can you do it backwards?

a b c d e f g h i j k l m n o p q r s t u v w x y z

A lot of otters wearing overalls
As hot as oven gloves
Trot off down to the river
Which is what an otter loves.

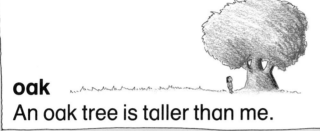

oak
An oak tree is taller than me.

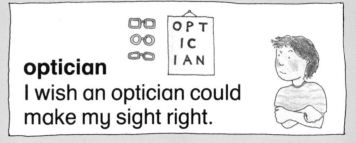

optician
I wish an optician could make my sight right.

oar
Paddle with a paddle or an oar.

orange
An orange is orange but this melon is lemon.

oats
Goats eat oats.

ostrich
An ostrich in a ditch.

ocean
Does the motion of the ocean make you ill?

otter
The otter has a lotta fun!

oil
I'll oil the engine.

owl
How'll the owl use a towel?

Oo

What do you get if you cross an owl with a skunk?

A bird that smells but doesn't give a hoot.

Can you make all these words from the letters on the octopus' legs?

red   bed   bear
ear   cat   rat
bat   dot   rot

How many more can you make?

a b c d e f g h i j k l m n o p q r s t u v w x y z

hiccup

Hiccup, Hiccup, Hiccup,
Goes the prickly porcupine
Supine after a super supper
Of pickles, pork pies and port wine.

panda
A panda and a gander

pelican
An American pelican

parachute
A parakeet in a parachute

pencil
Draw around a stencil
with a pencil.

parrot
The parrot pecked a carrot.

pineapple
A piece of pickled pineapple.

peach
Have a peach each.

pirate
Would you fire at a pirate?

peacock
As proud as a peacock

python
A python on a pylon

Pp

What do porcupines eat with cheese?

Prickled onions.

Can you copy like a parrot? Point to the matching words.

Goodbye
Hello
Pretty boy
Got any food?
Let me out

a b c d e f g h i j k l m n o p q r s t u v w x y z

Hey diddle diddle, here is a riddle
To puzzle out if you can.
What is found in a river (and ends in shiver)
Ring o' roses, red noses and Gran?

queen
The queen quickly asked a question.

rake
Can you make a cake with a rake?

queue
A queue for the boat

rhinoceros
A rhinoceros seems big to us.

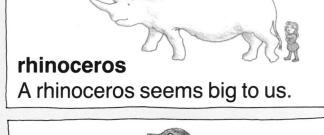

quilt
A patchwork quilt

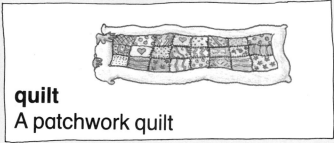

robin
A robin bobbing up and down

rabbit
A rabbit is nibbling a radish.

robot
Robert the robot

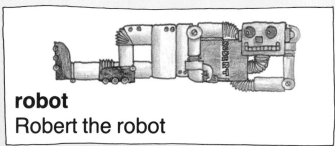

rainbow
Count the rainbow colours.

roller boots
Roll along on roller boots.

Qq Rr

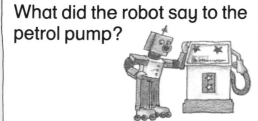

What did the robot say to the petrol pump?

Take your finger out of your ear when I'm talking to you.

The baby rabbit has got lost in his burrow. Which tunnel leads to his mother?

a b c d e f g h i j k l m n o p q r s t u v w x y z

Don't go sliding on the ice in your slippers
It's so slippery that certainly you'll slip
Put on a penguin suit and flippers
To be sure that you get the perfect grip.

sand-castle
A sand-castle at the seaside

skateboard
A skunk on a skateboard

sausage
A sausage in a saucepan

snail
A snail's silvery trail

scarecrow
A tattered and torn scarecrow

spider
I spied a spider.

seagull
Can you see a seagull?

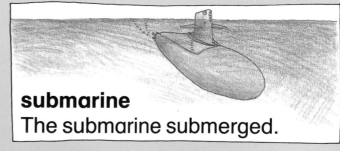

submarine
The submarine submerged.

sheep
Seven shaggy sheep
should be shorn.

swing
Will a king sing on a swing?

Ss

Tongue Twister:

The sixth sick sheik's sixth sheep's sick.

Can you find ten seaside things hidden in the seaweed?

a b c d e f g h i j k l m n o p q r s t u v w x y z

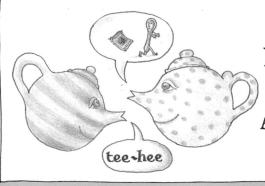

Don't put two teapots together
They will tittle ~ tattle like mad
About tea things like teabags and teaspoons
And the wonderful teatimes they had.

tee-hee

taxi
Elephants need a maxi taxi.

toad
A toad crossing the road

teddy bear
The teddy bear has lost its hair.

tractor
He backed the tractor up the hill.

telephone
A teeny-tiny tortoise
is on the telephone.

train
The train came and went again.

television
Cartoons on the television

tree
Can you see the bee in the tree?

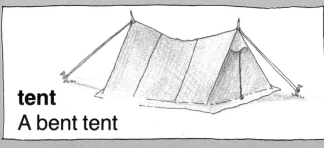

tent
A bent tent

tricycle
You could try a tricycle if you
fall off a bicycle.

Tt

What's yellow and white and travels at over 100 mph?

A train driver's egg sandwich.

Use the typewriter to type these words:

tap   tin   ten   top   tug   tea

a b c d e f g h i j k l m n o p q r s t u v w x y z

'Yuk!' says the yak, 'it tastes like spam,
Mother's home-made yellow yam jam.'
An ox exclaimed, 'Please give me a pot
The zebras at the zoo will soon scoff the lot.'

X-ray
He examined the
X-ray excitedly.

yoghurt
Yoghurt is yummy.

xylophone
A xylophone makes
a ringing tone.

yo-yo
Have a go-go on my yo-yo.

yacht
Have you got a yacht?

zebra
Debra the zebra

yak
A yak in a mac

zero
Three, two, one, zero
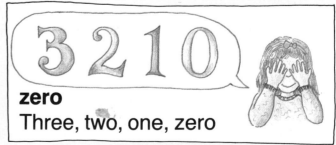

yellow
The yellow yolk of an egg

zoo
See a gnu at the zoo.

Xx Yy Zz

What is yellow and very dangerous?

Shark infested custard.

Match the footprints with the correct colour.

yellow
red
blue
green
orange